M000084175

GOOD NIGHT BROTHER

GOOD NIGHT BROTHER

Kimberly Burwick

Burnside Review Press   Portland, Oregon

Good Night Brother
© 2014 Kimberly Burwick

Cover Image: Esaias van Hulsen,
from *Zwartornament bestaande uit twee vlakken*, 1609

Cover Design: Regina Godfrey
Layout: Shira Richman

Printed in the U.S.A.
First Edition, 2014
ISBN: 978-0-9895611-4-3

Burnside Review Press
Portland, Oregon
www.burnsidereview.org

Burnside Review Press titles are available for purchase from the
publisher and Small Press Distribution (www.spdbooks.org).

For my son, Levi—the sowing time, the harvest, the always.

Good night brother I say to the water moccasin...

—Frank Stanford

Rings. Combs. Ghosts. Moths.
No one can find anything here.

—Radmila Lazić

In the lean fraction of distance between back barn
and the godfather moan of wind, dry volleying
of ruddy starlings and the forthright chord
that is both creek and birds of screech—
This is the pattern, the empty space of home,
the austerity and dissolve of light after quail sleep,
the real slavery of breathing such quiet rain.
We stay because we are good for the silence of horses,
break rock, break harvest in wood-weather,
in the cardboard stack beside the red prairie house.

Glory all the way to the trees, white lilacs
on cut grass, then nothing but the setting
flatness of short grains upon drifts of weeds.
I waste what stillness turns the decaying
robins bright, knowing you might live
longer than I wish, beyond the deaf
green paradise of home, longer than
the hanging lemons large enough
to tremble and sway. I've come to
believe you can't touch me, only the sun
letting go of terribly red ditches.

How could I have known that you
would sever the strict shimmering of all
green birds on snow—
each facing south-southwest
and the pine shaking seven seconds
in fog. In Exodus, water blooded
and boils broke forth, gassing like
some raw angel whose womb
would have been a soft song.
I see what you are by the way
you smell mother's tan neck.
Among us there is no counselor.

If we both are pleaders,
beggars in this sealed-up world
thank the one orange tree
in the unplanned landscape
there are finally birds between us.
Prairie is punishment for failings
but there is a certain kind of crime
that takes the matgrass months to know.
Every sentence is really a question of harvests.
Dawn among bridges of wheat, all
the weights and measures of cowfields.
I sink down into your odor
every time I remember mother's nightgown,
the way that cotton sharpened some
dark arcing in your strange, goblet eyes.
Without you it's simply blood pheasant,
silver pheasant, then night.

In the small hurricane the nests hold
in gilded branches, as milkweed is sometimes
caught in the suspended darker drafts.
Inside, you are making fun of moonlight,
sex with the teenage Catholic, anything to give
yourself the language of a miscarried psalm.
And who's to say I vowed to brass you
and balance you in the distant poppies.
The waste-places grow because
we cannot clot the rock sedge from
blooming its own blackness or you
from loving the organ of yourself.

Let's start with you
because you are the bolt
from the blue,
the positive flash
of anvil crawler
far from its parent
cloud. Your eyes are
weird remnants of lead,
corn-paths to
the pissed-on pinweed
far in a blur of bees.
I hear never
thunder but lightning
that follows me
into the red orchard
so past paradise
that fruits shine not.

Smell the son-of-a-bitch in the wintergreen field
riding the vines like pigs, so un-right even death
wants nothing to do with you.
Pale the erections of flowering spurge,
grass invisible to geese, moths too wet to rise
flicker and shake their way up moldy stone.
I think of shootings where blood is the true front
for pilgrimage, and come the green-eyed birds
to the body so blunt in its new white knowing.
But you are too wretched to waste on sin.
Milkweed shrivels and I
take my place among new flies.

It happens in the talus when sun firm
but far off spreads from lake water,
as if you sent two first lights, filling the
whole arc like Dickinson's burning robin
she named the red pilgrim almost grown
from dawn itself. I need to tell you
what passes between mountains,
in the yellow stints they call frostweed.
How they wept in perfect debris
for you to bend down and suspend
the unclean hours.

Always weather against the puritan thickets,
wheat-grains in the milk-stage against
only dust, some elegy raw
in the circling wind.
Friday, rain lashed the half-pound
rabbit, heaven-colored in the umbrage.
I want to have never known the loam
of you, the mortified border
between light rot and the white buds
of a sociopath opening the bathroom door.

The hoar weeds
have done
their summering.
It's time I say your
name out loud.
You who grew
nowhere wild and
still lace
the tender tale
of Autumn.
All of us wishing
the Lord's hurried
hand might settle
upon your large lips
and drag you
into the pen
of winter goats.

Empty yourself in the foamflower,
calla, the crushed chicory.
Greenflies nest in the blasted
bird, some blue-wing roadside
rots in the scrub beardtongue,
the hot air upon us to bear as is.
Some lay on warm ryegrass in
the last residue of cloud.
The geese go on being geese
silken in slashes of weather
whether we hammer them
to our wooden homes or not.
Tell us how this ends. In the throat,
the cloves, or in the dove coming
out of herself in the wayside seeds?

I see it only when horses are
in motion, the blur of canter
and lupine, muscle and prairie rock,
running the weeds in a condition of
quiet that is thunder tender
on dirt and thistle, on the bird-weeks
of April like a rain-born weeping
for the lost and cooling places I
roam just before moon.
Christ, the lambs are yellow
and the goats are rag paper. When I
watched you breathe on the virgin teen,
herons tried to feed their way
back to someone's normal soul.

The earth is through the lamb-farm
where sun bloods the apples,
where ticks in silence rest in the soak of backwater.
In the dream of your execution, I do
my violence with a green handkerchief,
birds shit on lavender, and the moon rises bald
and clean into the ditch. I hear the mental process
of silos simmer and the Pentecostal winds.
This house marked with snowberries and dust.
The great price of bringing forth wheat.

"THE OPPONENT IS DEATH IT IS ON A MOUNTAIN BY ITSELF"

—FRANK STANFORD

How the snow stays
in us, the first blizzard,
two acres of seminary
light almost wrapped
in its proffered gloss—
Let pass the voice of one
God only while we are young
and almond with the grace
of those we want gone.
Let the executed pink
of the downed peach
paper the loose air, the cedar
winds, ice-rains that doctor us,
our thousand-hour hearts like
leaf rot and sage.

DEFORMED

It's hard to know if I am side-walled
with vervain and leather-leaf or simply used
to the soft rush in the lower lives of
others, gray as you, clotted in your guttural
peace though in and out of your soiled mind.
I wait for a shadow of earth's bones today.
I take the trash to the edge of gravel
and watch other families grow
temple blue, downy and not deformed.
Can we not have the horror of your whole
soul this year, only the moldy breastbone
or maybe the crown.

What should come from
the red hawk lives on the limbs
of mother, the homeless lot
of stolen lilies, April and
the sway of creatures failing
on a windy night, the way waterflowers
damn us with their green apple
smells and brother rivers
himself toward you and the only
way to close his mouth
is to plug the throat with lilacs.

Again your body is staggering
in the phase-out
of the olive moths,
October of the grizzled petals
and one tree
all roughed-up and rootlets,
schlock maples here
and on the hill, polite
birch like a believer autumnal
but wasted by plains.
In the work of destruction
is the strange wash of intension,
hatches of winged ants,
the fresh monstrous wheat.
We sleep on the prairie—
with wants, with beastly wants.

SHAMPOO BOTTLE

In high school you and your friends went on
and on about a girl who had sex with her
shampoo bottle with a little help
from the boy she was with. You laughed harder,
using a plastic jug to imitate. But today the fainting
goats in the unreal green make you more
than odor and noise, like a farm animal who's left
this earth from licking too much spray on thistles.

SOFT FLIES DON'T SCAR THE BODY

All the voltaic cells
going east
up the mountain.
Some humid
afternoon like
this you'll know
the squabbling
of young things
born strangely,
in the balance and blank
strength of weather.
As you are ever aged
by the hush of certain
birds in the metallic
nesting trees
of no providence
and no true
continuing.

All the rabbits save us.
I find my way to them with parsley
ends thick in the oils of snow,
each shape flecked with
a blue-breathing glory,
an executed bewilderment
even I cannot skin.
I know there is a perfect paper
light in the belly of young things,
a high, dull earth melting,
butterflied for no reason.
Though I haven't mastered
the fragments—your coral
fingertips and suicide eyes,
the foolish virgins who take you
in and mouth-feed you
landscapes with oregano and
the right god.

The dark-veined rotor clouds
have no measure of the new purple
nettles hated across the valley newborn.
I am afraid again to get not far
enough from you, not the wheat-ends
of the long road, or to the mildew
of the perfect trees in the place
where harvest is the precise tissue
of glory. The hawk chases first the robin
then each starling in the begrimed willow.
O large the miracle of even that.

Not all the dust is carried down
by thunder, the leaden berries
trapped in the middle bushes,
in the waters and the once blistered lines
of shade and leaf. How much is found
on our leveled landscapes,
growing your goldenweed perfect
in the five weeks of lightning
pathless in the cold pollen
which winter loves
to deaden with blessing.
And damp is he who later
unbelts his gut and smells over
and over his large thumbs.

And the underbelly of convection clouds
become blossoms in their benumbed geometry
and the ground-blooms are rough-housed in the wind.
Scrub beardtongue crackles with no sound
and I use my cheek to touch them.
And where the birthing grass is raised
with white flowers, I toss my underclothes for good.
On a day when wrens are perfect carriers of light
am I wicked, I ask, am I wicked?

To give God the mist in them, trees at rest
in passion and starlings in green down
of sycamores. Everything blessed with utterance
either felled or falling. Nothing of our past is really
the strict minimum. The blight and raspberried
autumns, the shadblow and water quite near.
And if we become the stiff motion
of stars incarnate will we not cross
the moon eventually? I rest to disappear
the same bottomland scents that pass over
mowed grass, the coral decay of red ants.

The gift might be that taken are the trees
and jewelweed, the jack pine and water oak,
moccasin flowers wild but small. You've never
been able to stay through the great winds,
seeds come to you clean beyond act
and reward, water as if by the rule
that restrains it. I sleep on the last green
of the season. Pheasants close in on my body.

There were apples then
it was winter of teenage teeth,
breathing angels kissed wrongly
inside the mouth, diamond
clods of yourself down
your leg, on the basement
pool table, your friends
mounted and doomed
while birch-blown
I watched the never-green
soil take shape.

West, the height of orderly lupine
means that God would be closer
if he could. Like the red-washed finch
in low light on her blue eggs
filling out a world grained by
straight distance, whose sweetest clutch
is like those who have gone from sickness
to moths in their perishing fresh arcs.
Let me sit down in the woodchips
and tell you how to take a bath.
You must first lose two pounds of lilacs
and a mouthful of wet doves. You must eat
nothing but rye and blue joint grass.
Rain will come and it will not
be important.

You are the one who deserves the boils
on your face under wavelengths
of the UV lamp, sheets of collagen
film, scent of purple maples
sour in their strange matter
like pieces of snakeskin on June cement.
It doesn't matter what the sentences know.
Some say the day is dry with moths
which is true if we catch them whole and
fluttering to be rid of our pink, sweaty hands.

About the night,
about the kind of horses
feeding if not on spring
then on some graduated border
between the awful overtaking
of you and the very dove
who grows with me,
past your sickness and
into fields of straw
so past green, so delicate
they are the mind's rewording.
It's only natural, I tell father,
that the perverted starlings
go after other birds, the real
glory is the unprotected
lateness fiery as a blossomful
of lies.

A living bird smells of flies, loam in
the molded summer fields all petals and muck,
the awful slow-motion lark thrashing
the long grass, robin on the rock shaking rain.
You think the earth is growing past its borders—
black knapweed, ditch stonecrop, gray berries.
What you taste in the bottom of the pool
will nourish, will make sweeter the older rainwater
and oak, lilacs buried deep in the headlock
of grasses, birds and the hill almost sexual in its Fall weeping.
The words for a life more tilled than this are said but once.
The geese get older with us simply by flying away.

They say the brother will weep eventually.
They say surely he will come to you
another way like a hiker
in a long red version of summer
where lightning is cause enough
to lie down in the over-deathed wheat
in the wicked and wild streaks of
air blended with old-porch flowers.
Think of it, they say, he'll get the fetid
lime of lake rot or the misshapen legs
of wood stack frogs. And there will be two
kinds of night inside the blue cells of water.

All as the moths on mild nights
come freshly, as the sequence of shallow
storm colors brass the southern cuttings,
rain lash-tender hangs in the hazels
like the greater part of a sigh
for the serious flower so green
in spots even the grossly-made brother
pauses in a suck of quiet, his chunky
sides with landed gnats full of moments
they will never know as cold finch,
stunned blackbird, steel robin.

May, the seventy
seedlings lay patched
in the scotch
and hazel ground.
There was an art to
getting away
from you. Birch turned
to leathered fields.
I fed you to the green
river flies racing
between aspen
and eddy.
I shared
you with lightning
and laid you down
in the hole
of beauty where lily
mold and leaves
became sweet
with ants.

Canada geese and night herons over minted buds,
darkness and the bugs in silence.
There is no need to dwell on certainty this time,
when the tiny blue egg is un-fruited we hunt not
the single bird but the populous unnatural flock.
It's good to imagine your body blued and salted in earth,
glass-dead as blown marbles in hanging plants.
There is something in your temper of small pigs
in rain, the simple combination of warm slow
weather and the moon breathing hard come morning.

The crows are waxy and the vultures full of lead.
Insects on the road have gravel in their eyes,
apple fields unhinged from these two
hundred acres of hard red wheat.
The light on your plate will soon be winter-kill
and the green and sour sun is at an angle
of murder and quiet. The geese know it better.
Things change over a hill and come to us ashen.
If you want mother for your pleasure you'd better
have some bald teeth in that fire-throat of yours.
You'd better dip your thumbs in sycamore sap
and stamp your hands with iris juice so
there will be no question who is connected
to that dead-rabbit mind of yours.

No matter the sprouting
and translation
of greenery, I
see you always thieving
on humid roads
with the scent of
some desiccated badger,
your planet-red eyes
and thick arms petting
every dumb virgin
from here to Boston,
your name like a live
birth gone wrong.

It takes blindness to live with you
and white throats of sparrows.
The suckled and thickets with
birds sage and pure pattern.
I come through the meagerness
of viburnum and walk where
I want to walk, each season
a pulse on the land in requiem
for great sproutlands and partly
cut paths of the quivering natural.
Don't look so lonely. After death, love
is a place aplenty with gnats.

The rocket larkspur
and strange bird calls,
calla florid and wasted
in blue woods clouded
with this wish: heron ponds
and loops of garnet,
wild quiet of snowbrush
and my god, the glass buttes
as pincers that grace every
good girl with a lesser
distance, a safer cascade.

To the feast of errors
I give larch
that never bloom,
silk fishes of milkweed,
confusion of the divided seasons,
thorns in a pale nest blown
into pinecones.
Out of haying comes
the living light
as thistles, all who hate
you joined to you,
walking upright with
the strength of clean pine.

I am here for the wider
range seeds, the off-grid roads
left to hazel in a month
still quiet with once-needed
keys of maple, whole woods
flowering and clubbed by slow
wild birds who floating
are the flood of a heavy
patience misnamed grace.

I DO NOT LOVE

I have no more weights
for the nature of you, no fruited
weeds sweet briar red for
the fury you wild upon us.
Beneath aspen and larch
I calm in the new creations
of August. Always the storm
and shock of you bright-lifting
as bead lighting clears
to distant violet holes.

The blankest panic in these scrolls of dark,
pine needles sleepless in the one stroke
of headlights on wet, back roads
in a moonless week, the fresh strawfield
already forked and spiked though before you
walks something of a judge
with his fresh holes in the earth.
If our fictions are but unspoken names
aren't we only one bursting green family
cleaned then left for flies, aren't we together
the echo and the end of the echo?

The meadow large with lilies
drool on your lips, your oversized
thumbs in trees.
When love takes the form of
entropy the knees close and virgins
move water against fat kelp.
Think of the wind coming,
a front loader operation of moldy
earth, the pearl-drops of every
future genuinely full
of perversely stretched angels.

I saw the rape of August
water in seven fields that
grow only one wheat,
the stunned little amber
of the pleading hours
same as the self not out
of place but placed.
I was nothing that season.
A bitter floom with a bastard
brother stretched across town.
Though we will never suffer
because you fill your hands
with stinkbugs and wash
only the vision of your grand
overweened fists.

GREEN

It is fresh breath over larkspur
that is the final notice of order.
More than green sweet wind or
the hand with spit still on it.
Scored into scarlet is what we are.
Cut into September, arnicas and aster.
If there is a song left on this earth
with your name in it, I will raise it
high into every strict void.
And when the sinless bluebird's
nest is taken by wasps I will give
to God the second degree of grace.
Thus we are borne for the duration
of every poem.

ACKNOWLEDGMENTS

Grateful acknowledgment is made to the journals that have published the following poems, often in different versions:

Black Warrior Review: "We Are Where We Tremble" (Winner, *Black Warrior Review* Poetry Prize, 2011)

The Cortland Review: "What Began in Nineteen Sixty-Nine," "I Wish I Had a Photograph," "Red Pilgrim," "I Struggle with Your Breath," "'The Opponent Is Death It Is on a Mountain by Itself'"

Interim: "Panic Attack," "Reading the Cure for Imaginary Love" (originally published as "Reading the Gospel of Luke"), "And Scant Is the Newest Grace"

International Poetry Review: "And No Thief Approacheth and No Moth Corrupteth" (Winner, C.P. Cavafy Prize, 2011)

The Iowa Review: "The Sister," "The Therapists Say to Admit the Nature of You," "And Want Shall Shun You" (Runner-up, *Iowa Review* Award for Poetry, 2011)

Talking River: "July"

Kimberly Burwick is the author of *Has No Kinsmen* (Red Hen Press, 2006) and *Horses in the Cathedral*, winner of the Robert Dana Prize (Anhinga Press, 2011). She teaches creative writing at Washington State University and at UCLA Extension. Her poems have also won the C.P. Cavafy Prize from *Poetry International* and the *Black Warrior Review* Poetry Prize. Originally from New England, she now lives in Moscow, Idaho, with her husband and three-year-old son.